FORMAS

The Six Primary Doctrines of the Apostolic Faith

By

Daniel D. Bracamonte

WOLAC PUBLISHING
2825 Stockyard RD D6
Missoula, MT 59808

In Collaboration With
APOSTOLIC REVIEW PUBLISHING

First Edition

Dedicated to

the Church:

"But speak thou the

things which become

sound doctrine."

Titus 2:1

FOREWARD

When Pastor Bracamonte first presented the concept of this booklet to me, it felt like a lifelong prayer had been answered. As an evangelist and Bible study teacher, I am always in search of material that will make me a more skillful and fruitful soul winner. However, one of the longest-standing and most persistent problems I have encountered has remained unaddressed: the need for a Bible study so simple that it could be memorized and taught by a child. A Bible study that could flow off the tongue with just a split second's notice.

I was 14 years old the first time I was asked, "What do Apostolics believe?" I was stunned, not for lack of faith or knowledge of the scriptures, but for a simple and easy way to express the pillars of Apostolic doctrine. I am embarrassed to say that I was not as prepared for that moment as I could have been. However, that interaction played a pivotal role in motivating me to study the scriptures and be ready to give an answer to everyone. If only I had this booklet back then.

For me and many others, I believe FORMAS is the missing key. FORMAS will equip Apostolics around the world to convey the Apostles' doctrines quickly, thoroughly, and authoritatively. This will allow us not only to grow in our own faith but also in our ability to witness to the lost. Clarity breeds confidence. Pastor Bracamonte has made it incredibly plain; now all that remains is for us to run with it.

Some people will read this Bible study and think, "Why didn't I think of that first?" This is a testament to Pastor Bracamonte's diligence in study and unique style of communication. It is natural and organic. The ability to distill this much information into such a simple package shows not just a stroke of genius but an anointing to teach and a profound love for souls. I know I will be incorporating FORMAS into every Bible study I teach.

I am incredibly grateful that Pastor Bracamonte has made this resource available. I believe it will see widespread use. With this tool in hand, I believe that a new dawn of Apostolic evangelism is upon us. Let us work while it is day!

Rev. Tselot Kiefle
Founder, All Things Bible Study

FORMAS

QUESTIONS

What are the FORMAS?

It is a systematic method to help Apostolics understand, recall, and articulate the Apostolic Faith.

Where does the term FORMAS come from?

The term is derived from Romans 6:17 "that **FORM** of doctrine." In the Latin the term is translated as **FORMA.**

Is FORMAS an acronym?

Yes. Each one of the letters in the term **FORMAS** represents one of the six primary doctrines of the Apostolic Faith.

THE SIX FORMAS

Faith

One God

Resurrection

Mode of Salvation

Advents

Sanctification

DESCRIPTION

As you read through the key scriptures, notice, that both Paul and Jude emphasize the importance of adhering to a "form of doctrine (Rom. 6:17)" that was widely recognized (common, Jude 3) in the early church. This form of doctrine is so critical that the church is commanded to "teach no other doctrine (1 Tim. 1:3)."

The form of doctrine that both Paul and Jude refer to is what Luke describes as the "doctrine of the Apostles" (Acts 2:42). The Apostles' doctrine is the teaching that shaped the identity of the Apostolic community and defined their belief system. These six primary teachings are repeatedly emphasized throughout the New Testament, and are what I refer to as the FORMAS.

Are these six doctrines the only doctrines taught in the New Testament? The answer is no. The truth is, there are other doctrines present in the scriptures. However, the FORMAS are the six fundamental doctrines that were taught in the early church. There are other doctrines, such as the doctrine of Sin, the Church, the Holy Supper, and the Last Days, present in the New Testament. However many of these other New Testament doctrines either branch off from or are related to the FORMAS.

Ultimately, the goal of this booklet is to provide Apostolics with system to understand, recall, and articulate the six primary doctrines of the Apostolic faith; the FORMAS.

KEY SCRIPTURES

"But God be thanked, that ye were the servants of sin, but ye have obeyed from the heart that **form** of **doctrine** which was delivered you." Romans 6:17

"And they continued steadfastly in the apostles **doctrine** and fellowship, and in breaking of bread, and prayers." Acts 2:42

"As I besought thee to abide still at Ephesus, when I went into Macedonia, that thou mightest charge some that they teach no other **doctrine**." I Timothy 1:3

"Now I beseech you, brethren, mark them which cause divisions and offences contrary to the **doctrine** which ye have learned; and avoid them." Romans 16:17

"Beloved, when I gave all diligence to write unto you of the **common salvation**, it was needful for me to write unto you, and exhort you that ye should earnestly contend for **the faith** which was once delivered unto the saints." Jude 3

FORMA

I

FAITH

Root Scripture:

"But without faith it is impossible to please him: for he that cometh to God must believe that he is, and that he is a rewarder of them that diligently seek him."

Hebrew 11:6

Statement of Belief:

We believe in the necessity of faith because the scriptures teach us that "without faith it is impossible to please God." Without faith, no one can be saved.

BIBLICAL FAITH

We believe that faith is necessary, and that without faith no one can be saved (Rom. 2:8). Throughout the Bible, faith is projected as a crucial element in God's response to humanity. It is portrayed through the actions of men and women who believed God (Heb. 11:1-40).

God pleasing faith is illustrated by the writer of Hebrews when he points our eyes towards Abraham, "By faith Abraham when he was called to go out into a place which he should after receive for an inheritance, obeyed; and he went out, not knowing whither he went (Heb. 11:8)."

The duality of faith (belief and action) is emphasized by Abrahams obedient response towards God's instructions, he "obeyed; and he went out." Thus, faith, at least biblically, is much more than a mere intellectual belief in God. Biblical faith, the type of faith that is emphasized in the scriptures is better understood as a fusion of belief and obedient action (Jas. 2:18).

True faith is expressed in belief and action. In other words biblical faith demands that the one who believes responds in obedience to God's word. Indeed, obedient actions are the evidence of one's faith.

It is important to note that there is a type of faith that does not please God. In his letter to the twelve tribes, James states that the devils believe in God. Although the devils believe, their faith is dead (Jas. 2:19). The faith of devils is considered dead because it is not possible for devils to fuse their belief with obedient actions towards God.

James utilizes this illustration to teach the church that any faith that is void of obedient actions towards God is considered to be a "dead faith." James is simple and direct when he states, "that faith without works is dead (Jas. 1:20)." Thus, any faith that is not willing to respond in obedience to God's word is a devilish faith.

NOTES:

FORMA
II

ONE GOD

Root Scripture:

"Hear, O Israel: The Lord our God is one Lord: And thou shalt love the Lord thy God with all thine heart, and with all thy soul, and with all thy might."

Deuteronomy 6: 4-5

Statement of Belief:

We believe that there is only one God. The scriptures explicitly declare "The Lord our God is one." Because God is one singular being, He alone is worthy of worship.

ONE GOD

Like the early church in the book of Acts Apostolics believe in one God. This belief is referred to as monotheism. That there is only one God is a fundamental teaching in the Bible. The Old Testament scriptures repeatedly emphasize that the God of Israel, the God who created all things is one unique God.

The prophet Moses declared, "Unto thee it was shewed, that thou mightest know that the Lord he is God; there is none else beside him (Deut. 4:35)." Likewise, the prophet Isaiah speaking as the oracle of God says, "there is no God else beside me; A just God and a Saviour; there is none beside me. Look unto me, and be ye saved, all the ends of the earth: For I am God, and there is none else (Isa. 45:21-22)."

The very first commandment "thou shalt have no other gods before me (Exod. 20:3)" is based on the idea that the Israelite community understood that God is one singular being. In other words there are no other so-called gods. Therefore one who knows God is not to pray, worship, or sacrifice to any other gods, beings, or spirits. He or she is to be wholly devoted to the God who delivered them and blessed them. Thus, to believe in one God is to first believe no other gods exist, and second to love God with all of one's heart, mind, and strength (Deut. 6:5).

The same emphasis on the singularity of God is repeated throughout the New Testament. In the Gospel of Mark, Jesus quotes the Old Testament scriptures when he says, "The first of all commandments is, Hear, O Israel; the Lord our God is one Lord (Mark 12:29)."

The Apostle Paul stresses the oneness of God when he declares "Now unto the King eternal, immortal, invisible, the only wise God, be honour and glory for ever and ever. Amen (1 Tim. 1:17)." Paul further emphasizes the doctrine of one God when he states, "we know that an idol is nothing in the world, and that there is none other God but one (1 Cor. 8:4)."

The doctrine of one God is critical because it teaches us who to worship, it teaches that there are no other gods, and it teaches that God does not change (Mal. 3:6). This means that if God is one in the Old Testament, He is still one in the New Testament. Thus any claims that Jesus or the biblical writers make concerning the deity of Christ must fit within the doctrine of one God.

Thus, concerning Jesus Christ we must not attempt to fit him into some sort of human philosophical construct. Instead we must simply understand that the one God became a human person; the man Jesus Christ. The Apostle Paul teaches us that it is God who "was manifest in the flesh (1 Tim. 3:16)."

Notes:

FORMA
III

RESURRECTION

Root Scripture:

"For I delivered unto you first of all that which I also received, how that Christ died for our sins according to the scriptures; And that he was buried and that he arose again the third day according to the scriptures."

1 Corinthians 15:2-3

Statement of Belief:

We believe in the resurrection of Jesus from the dead. The scriptures teach us that he was crucified, buried, rose again, and was seen by many witnesses.

THE RESURRECTION

The validity of the Apostolic faith hinges on the reality of the resurrection. As the Apostle Paul states, "If Christ be not risen, then is our preaching vain, and your faith is also in vain (1 Cor. 15:14)." In other words, the gospel void of the resurrection is empty, meaningless, and powerless. If Jesus was not raised from the dead by the power of God, then the gospel—the message of the Bible—is reduced to nothing more than a mere fairy tale.

Indeed, the Apostolic hope of eternal life is rooted in the belief that Jesus Christ did rise from the dead and ascended into heaven. Thankfully, the Bible does not present a resurrection without witnesses. In fact, the scriptures record that not only did Peter and the Apostles give witness to the resurrection of Jesus Christ, but Paul also noted that over 500 followers of Jesus were able to testify to the Lord's resurrection (1 Cor. 15:6).

The Apostle Peter also bears record to the resurrection when he says, "For we have not followed cunningly devised fables, when we made know unto you the power and coming of our Lord Jesus Christ, but were eyewitnesses of his majesty (2 Pet. 1:16)."

While the resurrection is a real and historical event, for Apostolics, it is also a deeply spiritual and symbolic event. First, the resurrection affirms the Sonship of Jesus, Paul writes that Jesus was "declared to be the Son of God with power, according to the spirit of holiness, by the resurrection from the dead (Rom. 1:4)."

Likewise the resurrection is an affirmation of the deity of Christ. The Apostle Thomas upon seeing the risen Jesus cried out, "My Lord and my God (John 20:28)." In other words, the resurrection is a demonstration of the deity, the power, and Sonship of Christ. The resurrection declares that Jesus is Son, Lord, and God.

Further, the resurrection symbolizes Christ's victory over the power of death. In his very first sermon, Peter proclaims, "Whom God hath raised up, having loosed the pains of death: because it was not possible that he should be holden of it (Acts 2:24)."

Simply put, the scripture teaches us that death did not have the power to keep or hold the Lord Jesus in the grave. Paul states, 'Knowing that Christ being raised from the dead dieth no more; death hath no more dominion over him (Rom. 6:9)." Indeed, it is Jesus that declares, 'I am he that liveth, and was dead; and, behold, I am alive for evermore, Amen; and have the keys of hell and of death (Rev. 1:18).

The resurrection is the pinnacle of Christ's mission of salvation. If Jesus had not risen from the dead, we could not be saved, and we would still be in our sins (1 Cor. 15:17). Ultimately, the resurrection is a saving act; it is an act of grace and mercy on our behalf. On the cross, Christ simultaneously destroyed the power of sin and death. Paul writes that Jesus has "abolished death and hath brought life and immortality to light through the gospel (2 Tim. 1:10)." The cross is the payment for our sins, and the resurrection is the disarming of Satan's power.

For those who believe, the resurrection is two-fold: presently, we are resurrected spiritually, raised, as the Apostle Paul says into the "newness of life (Rom. 6:4)." Likewise, the resurrection serves as a token, or a guarantee, of our resurrection in the age to come. The scripture teaches us that those of us who have been buried in his death through baptism (Rom. 6:3), and sealed with his Spirit (Eph. 1:13) are assured that we will be raised bodily in the age to come.

Notice, what Paul says, "In a moment, in the twinkling of an eye, at the last trump: for the trumpet shall sound, and the dead shall be raised incorruptible, and we shall be changed. For this corruptible must put on incorruption, and this mortal must put on immortality (1 Cor. 15:52-53)." The physical resurrection promises a transformation of our bodies. While the specifics of our appearance remain a mystery, we are assured of one thing: we will be like the Lord, for "we shall see Him as He is (1 John 3:2)."

Notes:

FORMA
IV

MODE OF SALVATION

Root Scripture:

"Then Peter said unto them, Repent, and be baptized every one of you in the name of Jesus Christ for the remission of sins, and ye shall receive the gift of the Holy Ghost."

Acts 2:38

Statement of Belief:

We believe in the necessity of repentance, baptism for the remission of sins, and reception of the Holy Ghost with the evidence of speaking in other tongues as the Spirit gives evidence.

MODE OF SALVATION

What do we mean by "mode of salvation"? The word "mode" refers to the way or manner in which something occurs, is experienced, or is done. Therefore, when we use the phrase "mode of salvation," we are referring to the way someone is saved. Salvation means being saved from the wrath of God's impending judgment of mankind (Rom. 2:5-11). Indeed, all mankind will be judged because as the scripture declares, "All have sinned and come short of the glory of God (Rom. 3:23)."

We believe the biblical mode of salvation is clearly demonstrated in the book of Acts. On the day of Pentecost, the Apostle Peter commanded his listeners to "Repent, and be baptized every one of you in the name of Jesus Christ for the remission of sins, and you shall receive the gift of the Holy Ghost (Acts 2:38)." The result of Peter's sermon is that over 3000 people were baptized that same day. This same mode of salvation is repeatedly administered throughout the book of Acts.

Indeed, Peter's sermon demonstrates a harmony with the baptismal instructions of Jesus in Matthew 28:19. Jesus instructed the disciples to administer baptism in the NAME of the Father, Son, and the Holy Ghost. Indeed, that name is none other than Jesus. Paul confirms this when he tells the church that the "fulness of the Godhead (Col. 2:9)" dwells in Jesus.

It is important to note that salvation is only possible because of the death and resurrection of Jesus Christ. Salvation is not achieved by our own efforts; it is an act of faith in response to God's saving work for those who believe. As the Apostle Paul states, it is faith in the "operation of God" (Titus 2:12). This means that we do not provide the means for our own salvation; instead, we respond in faith to God's work. Repentance, Baptism, and the gift of the Holy Ghost are the call, work, and gift of God towards us. They should not be seen as our own works; rather, through faith, we willingly respond and participate in God's work within us.

REPENTANCE

Assuming one has faith in God and His Word, the first step towards salvation is repentance. Jesus emphasizes the urgency of repentance when He declares, "The time is fulfilled, and the kingdom of God is at hand: repent ye, and believe the gospel (Mark 1:15).

The word "repent" is a verb, meaning it is an action one must take to be saved. Repentance literally means to "think differently" or to change one's mind, purpose, or opinion. So, when God calls us to repent, He is asking us to change both our minds and our ways. Repentance is not optional; it is a crucial part of God's plan. Jesus said, "Except ye repent, ye shall all likewise perish" (Luke 13:3).

BAPTISM

Concerning baptism, Peter declares that it is for the "remission of sins" (Acts 2:38) and that it is the means of our salvation (1 Pet. 3:21). Biblically, baptism is a symbol representing the spiritual death and resurrection of the one being baptized. The Apostle Paul writes, "Therefore we are buried with him by baptism into death: that like as Christ was raised up from the dead by the glory of the Father, even so we also should walk in newness of life" (Rom. 6:4). Furthermore, baptism is associated with being planted into the crucifixion and death of Christ (Rom. 6:5-6).

Baptism directs us to a new spiritual reality and way of living. But we must not overlook the fact that it was instituted by the Lord Jesus (Luke 3:21-22) and is the only way one's sins can be washed away. Reflecting on his own experience, Paul reinforces the teaching that baptism washes away our sins when he writes, "And now why tarriest thou? Arise, and be baptized, and wash away thy sins, calling on the name of the Lord" (Acts 22:16).

Paul understood that baptism was more than a mere symbol by which we identify with Christ and His church. For the Apostle, baptism is both a symbol and the literal washing away of one's sins. It is the death of the old sinful person and the rebirth of a new spiritual creature in Christ Jesus (John 3:5; 2 Cor. 5:17).

Additionally, baptism is to be administered by calling on the name of the Lord, specifically the name of Jesus. Luke writes in the book of Acts, "Neither is there salvation in any other: for there is none other name under heaven given among men, whereby we must be saved" (Acts 4:12).

The Apostle Paul administered baptism in the name of Jesus. The scriptures tell us that when Paul found disciples of John the Baptist, he commanded them to be re-baptized "in the name of the Lord Jesus" (Acts 19:5). Upon being baptized, the disciples received the Spirit with the evidence of speaking in other tongues, affirming the correct mode of baptism (Acts 19:6).

One should keep in mind that baptism is not a work of the law or a work of the flesh by which one can earn salvation. On the contrary, the scriptures explicitly declare, "But when the goodness and loving kindness of God our Savior appeared, he saved us, not because of works done by us in righteousness, but according to his own mercy, by the washing of regeneration and renewal of the Holy Spirit" (Titus 3:5 ESV). "

In John 3:5, Jesus declares that unless "a man be born of water and of the Spirit, he cannot enter the kingdom of God." In this context, "the washing of regeneration" refers to water baptism, while "the renewing of the Spirit" refers to the infilling of the Holy Ghost. Classically, Apostolics have understood this as the fulfilment of what Jesus calls the born-again experience (John 3:3).

It's important to understand that baptism is not a work we perform to earn salvation; rather, it is a response of faith to the grace of God: "For the grace of God that brings salvation has appeared to all men" (Titus 2:11). As previously mentioned, the Bible teaches that baptism is not a human effort but "the operation of God" (Col. 2:12). Another translation describes it as "the powerful working of God" (ESV). Therefore, baptism represents our willingness to respond in faith to the Lord's call and His work within us.

One final note on baptism: the word "baptize" comes from the Greek word "baptizo," which literally means to immerse a person, thing or object in water. Historically, in the New Testament, baptism was performed by fully immersing the one being baptized into water. It is for this reason that Apostolic's continue to baptize in the same manner that the early church did in the book of Acts (Acts 8:36).

CALLING ON THE NAME

Luke not only stresses the necessity of baptism in water but also emphasizes calling on the name of the Lord. This call to salvation is prophesied in the Old Testament. The prophet Joel declares, "And it shall come to pass, that whosoever shall call on the name of the Lord shall be delivered" (Joel 2:32). In Acts 2:21, the Apostle Peter quotes Joel, saying, "And it shall come to pass, that whosoever shall call on the name of the Lord shall be saved." Scripturally, it is undeniable that calling on the name of the Lord (Jesus) is a critical component of salvation.

The Apostle Peter understood that calling on the name of the Lord was to be connected with baptism. This is why he commands the first believers to be "baptized in the name of Jesus" (Acts 2:38). For this reason baptism, along with water immersion, should include calling on the name of the Lord. Baptism in the name of Jesus is further validated when the house of Cornelius (Acts 10:48) and the disciples of John the Baptist (Acts 19:5) are commanded to be baptized in the name of the Lord Jesus.

One of the best examples of biblical baptism occurs in Acts 22:16. The Apostle Paul, testifying about his own baptismal experience rehearses how Ananias commanded him to be baptized, "And now why tarriest thou? arise, and be baptized, and wash away thy sins, calling on the name of the Lord." Clearly, Paul understood that salvation required baptism in Jesus' name for the remission of sins (Acts 2:38).

THE HOLY GHOST

As you read through the book of Acts, you will notice that the Spirt accompanied water baptism. In some cases the recipients received the Spirit before water baptism, while others received the Spirit after baptism (Acts 8:16; 10:44-48; 19:6). The scriptural emphasis is not on the sequence of reception (the order) but on the fact that Spirit baptism is a crucial part of God's plan. Indeed, Peter announces that the Spirit is a gift that is intended for all who believe (Acts 2:39).

The outpouring of the Spirit, like the birth of Jesus, is foretold throughout the Old Testament. For example, the prophet Isaiah declares, "For with stammering lips and another tongue will He speak to this people (Isa. 28:11)." In 1 Corinthians 14:21, Paul refers to this passage when instructing the church that speaking in tongues is a supernatural sign for those who believe.

The prophet Isaiah also declared that the Spirit would be poured out from on high (Isa. 32:15). Jesus referred to this prophecy when He told His disciples, "Behold, I send the promise of my Father upon you: but tarry ye in the city of Jerusalem, until ye be endued with power from on high" (Luke 24:49). On the day of Pentecost (Acts 2:1-4), Peter understood the outpouring of the Spirit to be the realization of the spiritual empowerment that Jesus promised to His disciples in Luke 24:49.

Another prophecy concerning the outpouring of the Spirit is found in Joel 2:28: "And it shall come to pass afterward, that I will pour out my spirit upon all flesh; and your sons and your daughters shall prophesy, your old men shall dream dreams, your young men shall see visions." When Peter declares, "This is that which was spoken by the prophet Joel" (Acts 2:16-17), he is pointing to the outpouring of the Spirit as the arrival of Joel's prophetic vision.

It's crucial to understand that the outpouring of the Spirit wasn't a singular event; it occurs repeatedly in the book of Acts and extends throughout the church's history.

Regarding the reception of the Spirit, five key points emerge. First, the baptism of the Spirit is a promise to those whom the Lord would call (Luke 24:49 Acts 2:38). Second, it is a baptism of fire that comes from above, and is administered by the Lord Jesus (Luke 24:49, Matt. 3:11). Third, the baptism of the Spirit is for spiritual empowerment (Acts 1:8). Fourth, the initial evidence/sign that the one has received the Spirit is speaking in other tongues as the Spirit gives utterance (Acts 2:4, 10:44-46, 19:6). Lastly, we must understand that the gift of the Spirit is something we must ask for. Luke tells us, "If ye then, being evil, know how to give good gifts unto your children: how much more shall your heavenly Father give the Holy Spirit to them that ask him?" (Luke 11:13).

Why do Apostolics place such an emphasis on Spirit reception? Because as Apostolics we believe that when the Lord fills anyone with the Spirit, at the same time he gives them a new heart. The prophet Ezekiel writes, "A new heart also will I give you, and a new spirit will I put within you: and I will take away the stony heart our of your flesh, and I will give an heart of flesh (Ezek. 36:26)."

Notice, it is the Spirit that heals a heart hardened by sin. The "stony heart" is literally transformed by the Spirit into a new heart that can receive the truth of God's word. The Apostle Paul summarizes: "Forasmuch as ye are manifestly declared to be the epistle of Christ ministered by us, written not with ink, but with the Spirit of the living God; not in tables of stone, but in fleshy tables of the heart (2 Cor. 3:30)."

Notes:

FORMA
V

ADVENTS

Root Scriptures:

"Behold, a virgin shall be with child, and shall bring forth a son, and they shall call his name Emmanuel, which being interpreted is, God with us."

Matthew 1:22

"For the Lord himself shall descend from heaven with a shout, with the voice of the archangel, and with the trump of God: and the dead in Christ shall rise first."

1 Thessalonians 4:16

Statement of Belief:

We believe in the two advents. The first advent is the incarnation; God appeared in the flesh as Jesus. The second advent is the return of Christ for His bride the church.

THE INCARNATION

The term "advent" comes from the Latin "adventus," meaning "appearance" or "coming." The "First Advent" is prophesied in the book of Isaiah: "For unto us a child is born, unto us a son is given: and the government shall be upon his shoulder: and his name shall be called Wonderful, Counsellor, The mighty God, The everlasting Father, The Prince of Peace (Isa. 9:6)."

The fulfillment of Isaiah's prophecy is recorded in the Gospels of Matthew 1:18-25 and Luke 1:26-35, 2:1-7. Both describe the birth of Jesus in supernatural terms. Matthew states that Mary "was found to be with child from the Holy Spirit" (Matt. 1:18 ESV). Luke records that the Spirit came upon Mary, and she gave birth to Jesus the Son of God (Luke 1:35).

Regarding the birth of Jesus, the prophet Isaiah declares, "A virgin shall conceive, and bear a son, and shall call his name Immanuel" (Isa. 7:14). In Matthew 1:23 the evangelist documents that the Lord, in a dream, spoke to Joseph regarding Isaiah's prophecy, telling him that Jesus would be called Emmanuel, and that he should interpret this to mean "God with us." In other words, the birth of Jesus Christ's is nothing less than the incarnation, the manifestation, the appearance of God to humanity in the flesh (John 1:14).

The Apostle John, unlike Matthew and Luke does not record the earthly birth of Jesus. Instead, John gives witness to the process of the Word (God) becoming flesh (human). In John 1:1 he states, "In the beginning the Word was the Word, and the Word was with God, and the Word was God." He then declares, "the Word was made flesh, and dwelt among us, (and we beheld his glory the glory as the only begotten of the Father), full of grace and truth (John 1:14)."

Clearly, John is describing the manner in which God came into the world. The eternal Word, the transcendent God, the eternal Spirit (John 4:24) took on the form of flesh, and became the man Jesus Christ. Again, John is describing the supernatural process, the manner in which God (the Word) came into the world. The Apostle Paul, describes this same process when he states, "And without controversy great is the mystery of godliness: God was manifest in the flesh (I Tim. 3:16)."

This process whereby God became a man is referred to as the "incarnation." The term "incarnation" refers to the "in-fleshing" of the Word. In-fleshing simply means that the divine God who is a Spirit (John 4:24) took on the form of flesh. More precisely, the "incarnation" is the process by which God became a human; Jesus the Son of God. Thus, the phrase "Fist Advent" is a term that describes the first coming, the entrance of God into the world through the virgin birth of Jesus.

THE SECOND COMING

The "Second Advent" refers to the second coming of Jesus Christ. We believe in the "Second Advent" because the Bible says, "Behold, he cometh with clouds; and every eye shall see him, and they also which pierced him: and all kindreds of the earth shall wail because of him. Even so, Amen" (Rev. 1:7). Regarding His second coming, Jesus says, "And then shall appear the sign of the Son of man in heaven: and then shall all the tribes of the earth mourn, and they shall see the Son of man coming in the clouds of heaven with power and great glory" (Matt. 24:30-31).

The second coming of Jesus Christ is a core teaching of the Apostolic faith. We believe He will return in power and glory for His church, and our hope is anchored in His promised imminent return. For this reason, Paul instructed the church to be "looking for that blessed hope, and the glorious appearing of the great God and our Savior Jesus Christ" (Titus 2:13).

We believe the "Second Advent" is a real and literal event that will mark the culmination of God's prophetic plan. It will be the moment that God returns as Jesus Christ to complete His redemptive work for His people and pour out His wrath on those who have rejected His truth (1 Thess. 1:10). It is important to note that the scriptures teach us that no man knows the day or hour of Christ's return. We are simply commanded to faithfully watch and hope for His second coming (Mark 13:32-33).

Notes:

FORMA
VI

SANCTIFICATION

Root Scripture:

"Follow peace with all men, and holiness, without which no man shall see the Lord."

Hebrews 12:14

Statement of Belief:

We believe in sanctification, because the Bible commands us to be holy like He is holy. We also believe that without holiness no one can see the Lord.

SANCTIFICATION

The terms "sanctification" and "holiness" are synonymous. Sanctification has two aspects: first, we are sanctified by what Christ has accomplished through His work on the cross, being made holy and set apart by His blood (1 Cor. 6:11). Second, we are called to participate in God's holiness by pursuing a godly and holy lifestyle (2 Cor. 7:1).

The Bible teaches us to be holy because God is holy: "It is written, Be ye holy; for I am holy" (1 Pet. 1:16). Thus, the call to holiness is rooted in God's nature. Because God is holy, we are called to be holy as well. Holiness involves aligning our lives with God's will and reflecting godliness in our character and actions. Additionally, holiness is a form of worship unto God, the Psalmist declares: "O worship the Lord in the beauty of holiness" (Ps. 96:9).

Lastly, the Bible warns that without holiness, no one can see the Lord (Heb. 12:14). Initially, we are made holy and sanctified through the blood of Christ. We must be made holy because God is holy, and without holiness, we cannot be in right relationship with Him.

Therefore, when God saves and restores us, He makes us holy so we can be in communion with Him. He also fills us with His Spirit to empower us to live a holy and pleasing life. Indeed, one of the primary reasons He indwells us is to help us maintain a right relationship with Him.

Notes:

PUTTING IT ALL TOGETHER

There are three ways to use this booklet. The first is to use it to become proficient in basics of the Apostolic doctrine. The second is to use it as way giving a Bible study to someone who desires to know more about the Apostolic faith. Lastly, and most importantly it should be used to help you articulate your faith in quick, intelligent and concise manner; an elevator pitch.

What is an elevator pitch? An elevator pitch is a brief way to introduce yourself, or to get a point across. In this case it is a quick way to introduce your Apostolic faith. It's called an elevator pitch because it takes roughly the amount of time you'd spend riding an elevator with someone (think 30 seconds) to explain the Apostolic belief system (doctrine).

If you happen to bump into someone who is open to you sharing your faith, but they are limited on time, how will you introduce yourself, how will you sum up your faith, and how will you get connected before you or that person runs out of time?

The answer is to have an elevator pitch, a system where you can recall, and articulate your Apostolic faith. This booklet, the FORMAS is an extremely effective tool for developing a concise elevator pitch; it is designed to help you share your faith confidently.

THE PITCH

We believe in the necessity of **F**aith, in **O**ne God, and the **R**esurrection of Jesus from the dead. We believe that Acts 2:38 is the biblical **M**ode of Salvation. We believe in the two **A**dvents, that is Jesus Christ is God manifest in the flesh, and that He will return for His church. Finally, we believe that through the power of the Holy Spirit, the Lord empowers us to live a **S**anctified life.

CONCLUSION

The most effective way to learn the FORMAS acronym is through repeated rehearsal. Use FORMAS as a trigger for each doctrinal point: "FORMAS, F is for Faith, O is for One God, R is for Resurrection, M is for Mode of Salvation, A is for Advents, and S is for Sanctification." You will be surprised at how quickly and confidently you can articulate your belief system.

Once you have mastered the acronym, move on to the elevator pitch. Take time to make it your own; it doesn't have to sound exactly as written. The key is to share your faith clearly and concisely, without fumbling through unnecessary words or ideas. If you get stuck, just repeat the acronym "FORMAS" to yourself.

You may want to use the term FORMAS when witnessing. I have used it to pique the curiosity of those I'm speaking with. When someone asks what I believe, I often reply with the term "FORMAS," and inevitably they ask, "What's that?" This gives me the chance to summarize what Apostolics believe. More often than not, they are open to a deeper explanation.

Remember, this is not a new theological system. It is simply a tool to help us communicate our faith in a systematic and sensible way. I pray this tool is useful in your Apostolic witness.

About the Author

Pastor Daniel Bracamonte has dedicated over three decades to teaching and preaching the Word of God. As the current Pastor of Word of Life, a thriving Apostolic church in Missoula, Montana, he has been instrumental in guiding the spiritual growth of his congregation. Daniel holds a Bachelor of Arts in Biblical Studies from Regent University in Virginia Beach, VA, and a Master of Theological Studies (MTS) in Biblical Studies from Regent School of Divinity. His passion for for Apostolic Doctrine, Biblical scholarship and Apostolic ministry continues to inspire and impact those he serves.